National Academy of Design (U.S.)

Loan Exhibition of Portraits

For the Benefit of St. John's Guild and the Orthopaedic Hospital

National Academy of Design (U.S.)

Loan Exhibition of Portraits
For the Benefit of St. John's Guild and the Orthopaedic Hospital

ISBN/EAN: 9783337163051

Printed in Europe, USA, Canada, Australia, Japan

Cover: Foto ©ninafisch / pixelio.de

More available books at **www.hansebooks.com**

LOAN EXHIBITION

OF

PORTRAITS

FOR THE BENEFIT OF

ST. JOHN'S GUILD AND THE

ORTHOPÆDIC HOSPITAL

FROM THE THIRTIETH OF OCTOBER TO

THE SEVENTH OF DECEMBER, MDCCCXCV

NATIONAL ACADEMY OF DESIGN
CORNER OF FOURTH AVE. AND TWENTY-THIRD ST.
NEW YORK

The Knickerbocker Press, New Rochelle, N. Y.

EXECUTIVE COMMITTEE.

HENRY MARQUAND, Chairman,
E. HAMILTON BELL, Secretary
OSGOOD WELSH, Treasurer,
JAMES SPEYER,
CHARLES T. BARNEY,
WILLIAM F. KING,
H. WALTER WEBB,
ROBERT WALLER, Jr.

LADIES' COMMITTEE.

Mrs. ROBERT B. POTTER,
Mrs. HENRY WINTHROP GRAY,
Mrs. JOHN A. LOWERY,
Mrs. CHARLES de RHAM, Jr.,
Mrs. J. HOBART WARREN,
Mrs. ADOLF LADENBURG,
Mrs. M. DWIGHT COLLIER.

ARTISTS' COMMITTEE.

FRANCIS LATHROP, Chairman
J. CARROLL BECKWITH,
WILLIAM M. CHASE,
H. SIDDONS MOWBRAY,
BENJAMIN C. PORTER,
STANFORD WHITE,
EASTMAN JOHNSON.

PATRONESSES.

Mrs. CHARLES B. ALEXANDER.
Mrs. A. A. ANDERSON.
Mrs. ASTOR.
Mrs. JOHN JACOB ASTOR.
Mrs. EDMUND L. BAYLIES.
Mrs. JOHN N. BEEKMAN.
Mrs. GEORGE H. BEND.
Mrs. EDWARD J. BERWIND.
Mrs. ARTHUR BIRD.
Mrs. GEORGE S. BOWDOIN.
Mrs. JAMES LAWRENCE BREESE.
Mrs. WILLIAM LANMAN BULL.
Mrs. JAMES ABERCROMBIE BURDEN.
Mrs. A. CASS CANFIELD.
Mrs. HENRY CLEWS.
Mrs. M. DWIGHT COLLIER.
Mrs. STUART A. COATS.
Mrs. AUSTIN CORBIN.
Mrs. ELLIOT C. COWDIN.
Mrs. JOHN E. COWDIN.
Mrs. RALSTON CROSBY.
Mrs. VAN RENSSELAER CRUGER.
Mrs. WILLIAM BAYARD CUTTING.
Mrs. ROBERT FULTON CUTTING.
Mrs. PAUL DANA.
Mrs. WILLIAM STARR DANA.
Miss CAROLINE DE FOREST.
Mrs. GEORGE B. DE FOREST.
Mrs. ROBERT W. DE FOREST.
Mrs. WARREN E. DENNIS.
Mrs. WILLIAM BUTLER DUNCAN.
Mrs. ELISHA DYER, Jr.
Mrs. HAMILTON FISH.
Mrs. FREDERIC DE PEYSTER FOSTER.
Mrs. ROBERT LUDLOW FOWLER.
Mrs. CHARLES G. FRANCKLYN.
Mrs. GEORGE A. FREEMAN.
Miss FRELINGHUYSEN.
Miss FURNISS.
Mrs. RICHARD WATSON GILDER.
Mrs. ROBERT GOELET.
Mrs. H. W. GRAY.
Miss HAMILTON.
Mrs. ALFRED S. HEIDELBACH.
Miss HEWITT.
Mrs. THOMAS HITCHCOCK.
Mrs. GEORGE HOFFMAN.
Miss HOFFMAN.
Mrs. HARRY B. HOLLINS.
Mrs. HENRY HOLT.
Mrs. JOHN HONE.
Mrs. RICHARD IRVIN.
Mrs. WILLIAM E. ISELIN.
Mrs. WILLIAM JAY.
Mrs. MORRIS K. JESUP.
Mrs. FREDERIC RHINELANDER JONES.
Mrs. DE LANCEY A. KANE.
Mrs. ADOLF LADENBURG.
Mrs. CHARLES LANIER.
Mrs. F. M. LATHROP.
Mrs. EDWARD LAUTERBACH.

PATRONESSES.

Mrs. BENONI LOCKWOOD.
Mrs. GEORGE B. LORING.
Mrs. PIERRE LORILLARD, Jr.
Mrs. JOHN A. LOWERY.
Mrs. E. LIVINGSTON LUDLOW.
Mrs. HENRY MARQUAND.
Miss MARIA D. B. MILLER.
Mrs. JOHN W. MINTURN.
Mrs. J. PIERPONT MORGAN.
Mrs. RICHARD MORTIMER.
Mrs. STANLEY MORTIMER.
Mrs. LEVI P. MORTON.
Mrs. JORDAN L. MOTT, Jr.
Mrs. J. ARCHIBALD MURRAY.
Mrs. THOMAS NEWBOLD.
Mrs. HENRY FAIRFIELD OSBORN.
Mrs. WM. CHURCH OSBORN.
Miss PARSONS.
Mrs. ROBERT B. POTTER.
Mrs. GEORGE RUTLEDGE PRESTON.
Mrs. CHARLES de RHAM, Jr.
Mrs. GEORGE L. RIVES.
Mrs. J. HAMPDEN ROBB.
Mrs. HENRY ASHER ROBBINS.
Mrs. DOUGLAS ROBINSON, Jr.
Mrs. WILLIAM ROBISON.
Mrs. JAMES A. ROOSEVELT,
Mrs. JACOB H. SCHIFF.
Mrs. PHILIP SCHUYLER.
Mrs. GUSTAV H. SCHWAB.
Mrs. FREDERICK SHELDON.
Mrs. WILLIAM WATTS SHERMAN.
Mrs. SAMUEL SLOAN.
Mrs. WILLIAM DOUGLAS SLOANE.
Mrs. BYAM K. STEVENS.
Mrs. WILLIAM RHINELANDER STEWART.
Mrs. ANSON PHELPS STOKES.
Mrs. ARTHUR MURRAY SHERWOOD.
Mrs. JOSEPH STICKNEY.
Mrs. MARION STORY.
Mrs. WILLIAM E. STRONG.
Mrs. WILLIAM L. STRONG.
Mrs. OLIVER SUMNER TEALL.
Mrs. J. KENNEDY TOD.
Mrs. SPENCER TRASK.
Mrs. HAMILTON McK. TWOMBLY.
Mrs. CORNELIUS VANDERBILT.
Mrs. FREDERICK W. VANDERBILT.
Mrs. ALEX. VAN RENSSELAER.
Mrs. S. WHITNEY WARREN.
Mrs. J. HOBART WARREN.
Mrs. H. WALTER WEBB.
Mrs. W. SEWARD WEBB.
Mrs. HAMILTON FISH WEBSTER.
Mrs. SIDNEY WEBSTER.
Mrs. STANFORD WHITE.
Mrs. PENNINGTON WHITEHEAD.
Miss WHITNEY.
Mrs. BUCHANAN WINTHROP.
Mrs. FREDERICK WISSMANN.

CATALOGUE.

ABBREVIATIONS.

C.—Corridor.   S.—South Gallery.
N.—North Gallery.   E.—East Gallery.
W.—West Gallery.

PORTRAITS.

FRANCIS ALEXANDER.

1. N. P. Willis.   N.
   Lent by MRS. GRINNELL WILLIS.

JOHN W. ALEXANDER.

2. Portrait.   W.
   Lent by JOHN W. ALEXANDER, ESQ.

3. James W. Alexander.   E.
   Lent by JOHN W. ALEXANDER, ESQ.

4. Portrait. E.
   Lent by J. RANDOLPH COOLIDGE, Esq., Jr.

5. James W. Alexander, Jr. S.
   Lent by JOHN ALEXANDER, Esq.

FISHER AMES.

6. Judge Levi Beardsley. N.
   Lent by Mrs. E. BEARDSLEY VAN DE WATER.

A. A. ANDERSON.

7. Princesse de W. C.
   Lent by A. A. ANDERSON, Esq.

GEORGE A. BAKER, 1821–1880.

8. Mrs. Edward Delafield. S.
   Lent by Mrs. HOWARD CLARKSON.

9. Mrs. S. P. Avery. W.
   Lent by S. P. AVERY, Esq.

10. Ellen Walters Avery. S.
    Lent by S. P. AVERY, Esq.

11. S. Oakley Van der Poel, M.D., LL.D.   C.
    Lent by MRS. G. W. VAN DER POEL.

12. Mrs. S. Oakley Van der Poel.   C.
    Lent by MRS. G. W. VAN DER POEL.

13. Portrait.   N.
    Lent by MRS. NATHAN CLARK.

CECILIA BEAUX.

14. Master Percival Drayton Taylor.   C.
    Lent by MRS. J. MADISON TAYLOR.

15. Child's Head.   S.
    Lent by MRS. R. H. HARTE.

CARROLL BECKWITH.

16. John Murray Mitchell, Esq.   S.
    Lent by THE FENCERS' CLUB OF N. Y.

17. Mrs. Anson R. Flower.   E.
    Lent by ANSON R. FLOWER, ESQ.

18. Miss Edith Poor.   S.
    Lent by HENRY W. POOR, ESQ.

19. Mrs. Davis. S.
  Lent by JOHN W. A. DAVIS, Esq.

20. Miss Anna Murray Vail. S.
  Lent by CARROLL BECKWITH, Esq.

21. Child. W.
  Lent by CARROLL BECKWITH, Esq.

A. A. BEEBE.

22. Dr. Lewenberg.
  Lent by DR. LEWENBERG.

23. Mrs. Newton Dexter.
  Lent by MRS. NEWTON DEXTER.

ELEANOR BELL.

24. Mrs. Henry Villard. W.
  Lent by MRS. HENRY VILLARD.

JEAN JOSEPH BENJAMIN-CONSTANT.

25. Mrs. Samuel W. Bridgham. W.
  Lent by WM. C. SCHERMERHORN, Esq.

26. Mrs. Daniel Chauncey. E.
   Lent by DANIEL CHAUNCEY, JR., ESQ.

F. E. BERTIER.

27. Mrs. Kingdon. C.
   Lent by MRS. GEORGE JAY GOULD.

EDWIN H. BLASHFIELD.

28. Mrs. George Hoffman. S.
   Lent by MRS. GEO. HOFFMAN

LEON BONNAT.

29. R. Fulton Cutting. W.
   Lent by R. FULTON CUTTING, ESQ.

30. Wm. Bayard Cutting. W.
   Lent by WM. BAYARD CUTTING, ESQ.

31. Hon. Levi P. Morton. S.
   Lent by HON. LEVI P. MORTON.

BRAGGAR.

32. Junius S. Morgan. W.
   Lent by J. PIERPONT MORGAN, ESQ.

ROBERT D. BRAINARD.

33. Dudley S. Carpenter.   E.
    Lent by MAJ. G. S. CARPENTER.

MISS MARIA BROOKS.

34. Miss Renée H. Weeks.   W.
    Lent by WM. R. WEEKS, ESQ.

35. Miss Rundel.   C.
    Lent by MISS MARIA BROOKS.

36. Rev. Reuben W. Howes, D.D.   E.
    Lent by REV. REUBEN W. HOWES, D.D.

37. Rev. Morgan Dix, D.D.   C.
    Lent by REV. MORGAN DIX, D.D.

GEORGE DE FOREST BRUSH.

38. Boy.   S.
    Lent by GEORGE DE FOREST BRUSH, ESQ.

39. Henry George.   E.
    Lent by AUGUST LEWIS, ESQ.

MRS. M. LESLIE BUSH-BROWN.

40. Miss P.   E.
Lent by M. P. JACOBI, Esq.

GEORGE B. BUTLER.

41. Mrs. Jane M. Miller.   C.
Lent by CHARLES H. MILLER, Esq.

42. Portrait Study, "The Grey Girl."   S.
Lent by Mrs. L. T. HAGGIN.

43. Portrait.   S.
Lent by Mrs. L. T. HAGGIN.

44. Portrait.   S.
Lent by Miss BREESE.

HOWARD RUSSELL BUTLER.

45. George E. Munroe, M.D.   E.
Lent by GEORGE E. MUNROE, M.D.

ALEXANDRE CABANEL, 1823–1889.

46. Family Group.   W.
Lent by J. W. PINCHOT, Esq.

PIERRE CABANEL.

47. Boy.   C.
   Lent by J. W. PINCHOT, Esq.

GEORGINE CAMPBELL.

48. Sister of the Artist.   C.
   Lent by Miss GEORGINE CAMPBELL.

CARNAVARI.

49. Mrs. John Jay (aged 12).   N.
   Painted in Rome, 1831.
   Lent by WILLIAM JAY, Esq.

JOHANNES CARRÉ, 1698–1772.

50. Lady.   N.
   Lent by WILLIAM MACBETH, Esq.

ANNA MEIGS CASE.

51. Meigs Case, M.D.   W.
   Lent by MEIGS CASE, M.D.

52. Madame Vitti.
   Lent by Miss A. MEIGS CASE.

MARY CASSATT.

53. Child.   C.
   Lent by PROF. WM. M. SLOANE.

LESLIE CAULDWELL.

54. Miss Livor.   C.
   Lent by DR. LIVOR.

55. Mrs. R. U. Johnson.   C.
   Lent by R. U. JOHNSON, ESQ.

JAMES WELLS CHAMPNEY.

56. Mrs. Frank S. Witherbee and Children.   C.
   Lent by MRS. F. S. WITHERBEE.

57. Mme. de Pompadour, after Latour.   C.
   Lent by JAMES WELLS CHAMPNEY, ESQ.

CHARLES J. CHAPLIN.

58. Harold Vanderbilt.   S.
   Lent by MRS. W. K. VANDERBILT.

THEOBALD CHARTRAN.

59. Little Miss Sloane. S.
    Lent by HENRY T. SLOANE, Esq.

60. Calvé (in Carmen). E.
    Lent by M. KNOEDLER & CO.

61. Pope Leo XIII. S.
    Lent by M. KNOEDLER & CO.

62. Portrait. W.
    Lent by AUGUST BELMONT, Esq.

63. Portrait. W.
    Lent by AUGUST BELMONT, Esq.

WILLIAM MERRITT CHASE.

64. E. G. Kennedy. S.
    Lent by E. G. KENNEDY, Esq.

65. Alice Dieudonnée Chase. S.
    Lent by WM. M. CHASE, Esq.

66. Little Miss C. S.
    Lent by WM. M. CHASE, Esq.

67. Mrs. C. S.
    Lent by WM. M. CHASE, Esq.

68. Miss E.   S.
   Lent by WM. M. CHASE, Esq.

69. James McNeil Whistler.   S.
   Lent by WM. M. CHASE, Esq.

70. Mrs. G.   E.
   Lent by JOHN R. GLENNY, Esq.

71. Dr. Mundé.   W.
   Lent by Mrs. MUNDÉ.

72. My Sister.   C.
   Pastel.
   Lent by WM. M. CHASE, Esq.

MARIE CHAUCHEFOIN.

73. The Cherry Girl (copy of Picture in the Louvre).   C.
   Lent by Mrs. J. WELLS CHAMPNEY.

FRANÇOIS CLOUET, 1510–1572.

74. Charles of France, Son of Francis I.   N.
   Lent by GEORGE A. HEARN, Esq.

75. The Brother of Claude De Clermont.   N.
   Lent by T. J. BLAKESLEE, Esq.

76. Portrait. N.
    Lent by WM. M. CHASE, ESQ.

GEORGE RENLING COLE.

77. Mrs. Potter Palmer. W.
    Lent by MRS POTTER PALMER.

78. Mrs. H. G. Lord. E.
    Lent by L. W. LORD, ESQ.

JOHN SINGLETON COPLEY, 1737–1815.

79. Henry Ludlow. N.
    Lent by JAMES B. LUDLOW, ESQ., and others.

80. Frances Duncan (wife of Henry Ludlow). N.
    Lent by JAMES B. LUDLOW, ESQ., and others.

81. Girl with Doves. N.
    Lent by D. F. APPLETON, ESQ.

82. Josiah Eliot. C.
    Pastel.
    Lent by J. SANFORD SALTUS.

MRS. LESLIE COTTON.

83. Miss Winslow. E.
    Lent by MRS. LESLIE COTTON.

84. Mrs. Albert Stevens. C.
    Lent by MRS. ALBERT STEVENS.

85. Mrs. Lucius Wilmerding. C.
    Lent by MRS. LUCIUS WILMERDING.

86. Child. C.
    Lent by HUGH COTTON, ESQ.

87. Child. C.
    Lent by HUGH COTTON, ESQ.

88. S. M. Roosevelt. E.
    Lent by S. M. ROOSEVELT, ESQ.

89. Mrs. Leslie Cotton. C.
    Lent by MRS. LESLIE COTTON.

LOUISE COX.

90. Mrs. S. W.
    Lent by FRANCIS M. SCOTT, ESQ.

CHARLES C. CURRAN.

91. Mrs. Savidge. C.
    Lent by DR. EUGENE COLEMAN SAVIDGE.

92. The Artist's Parents. C.
    Lent by MRS. E. E. THOMPSON.

H. DARBY.

93. Virginia Darby Ver Planck and E. Ver Planck.   E.
Lent by MRS. V. D. VER PLANCK.

94. Portrait Study, " Red Riding Hood."   E.
Lent by MRS. V. D. VER PLANCK.

THOMAS DE KEYSER, 1596–1679.

95. A Burgomaster and his Family.   N.
Lent by WILLIAM MACBETH, ESQ.

96. Group.   N.
Lent by WM. M. CHASE, ESQ.

JUAN KEATS DE LLANOS.

97. Fanny Keats de Llanos.   N.
Lent by MRS. J. G. SPEED.

PERCIVAL DE LUCE.

98. Child.   W.
Lent by PERCIVAL DE LUCE.

G. DE MARÉE, 1697–1776.

99. Carl IV., Prince Elector of the Palatinate-
Bavaria, 1742–1799.   N.
Lent by B. N. ZELLER.

FRANÇOIS DETROY.

100. Marquise de Louvois.   N.
Lent by EDWARD BRANDUS, ESQ.

MRS. CHARLES M. DEWEY.

101. Child.   S.
Lent by DR. GORHAM BACON.

T. W. DEWING.

102. Wm. M. Chase.   W.
Lent by WM. M. CHASE, ESQ.

M. R. DIXON.

103. Miss D.   C.
Lent by H. T. MAC CONNELL, ESQ.

GERARD DOW, 1613-1675.

104. Young Man. N.
Lent by GEORGE A. HEARN.

FRANÇOIS HUBERT DROUAIS, 1727-1775.

105. Madame d'Orleans. N.
Lent by EDWARD BRANDUS, Esq.

SAMUEL DRUMMOND, 1763-1844.

106. Portrait. N.
Lent by Mrs. CANDACE WHEELER.

ASHER B. DURAND.

107. Mrs. Nicholas Wm. Stuyvesant, *née* Katherine Livingston Reade. N.
Lent by HENRY DUDLEY, Esq.

CAROLUS DURAN.

108. Miss Consuelo Vanderbilt. S.
Lent by Mrs. W. K. VANDERBILT.

109. Mrs. George Jay Gould. S.
Lent by GEORGE J. GOULD, Esq.

0. Mrs. J. C. Ayer. W.
   Lent by FRED. F. AYER, Esq.

1. Mrs. Calvin S. Brice and her Daughters. W.
   Lent by CALVIN S. BRICE, Esq.

R. E. W. EARLE.

2. Andrew M. Jackson, President U. S. N.
   Lent by V. G. FISCHER ART CO.

CHARLES LORING ELLIOTT, 1812–1868.

3. Mrs. George Hunt. S.
   Lent by F. R. KALDENBERG.

4. S. P. Avery. W.
   Lent by S. P. AVERY, Esq.

5. N. P. Willis. C.
   Lent by MORRIS PHILLIPS, Esq.

6. Edwin Forrest. W.
   Lent by STILSON HUTCHINS, Esq.

7. James S. Mitchell. W.
   Lent by Mrs. J. S. MITCHELL.

ELIZABETH EMMETT, 1810.

118. Mrs. Thompson.   N.

Lent by THOMAS ADDIS EMMET, M.D.

LYDIA FIELD EMMET.

119. Charles de Rham, 3d.   C.

Lent by Mrs. CHARLES DE RHAM, JR.

LEON Y ESCOSURA.

120. Portrait of Himself.   E.

Lent by S. P. AVERY, ESQ.

FAGNANI.

121. Mrs. Edward Renshaw Jones.   E.

Lent by MRS. E. R. JONES.

J. COLIN FORBES.

122. Norman Forbes.   E.

Lent by J. COLIN FORBES, ESQ.

FRANK FOWLER.

123. Mrs. B.   S.

Lent by FRANK FOWLER, Esq.

KENNETH FRAZIER.

124. Bishop of Albany.   S.

Lent by KENNETH FRAZIER, Esq.

125. A Baby.   C.

Lent by RUDOLPH E. SCHIRMER, Esq.

THOMAS GAINSBOROUGH, 1727-1788.

126. Princess Charlotte.   N.

Lent by JAMES P. CLOHERTY, Esq.

127. Richard B. Sheridan.   N.

Lent by D. F. APPLETON, Esq.

FRANÇOIS PASCAL GERARD (attributed to) 1770-1837.

128. Emperor Napoleon I.   N.

Lent by EDWARD BRANDUS, Esq.

H. GOELET.

129. Child.   W.
Lent by STANFORD WHITE, Esq.

G. GORDIGIANI.

130. Mrs. Charles B. Alexander.   C.
Lent by Mrs. C. B. ALEXANDER.

131. Mrs. John Cropper, *née* Anne McLane, 1883.
W.
Lent by JOHN CROPPER, Esq.

ELIOT GREGORY.

132. "A Muse"—Miss Lillian Russell.   C.
Lent by ELIOT GREGORY, Esq.

JEAN BAPTISTE GREUZE, 1725–1805.

133. Child's Head.   N.
Lent by CORNELIUS VANDERBILT, Esq.

S. J. GUY.

134. "Solitaire," a Portrait.   W.
Lent by Miss FALCONER.

135. "Evening," a Portrait. W.
Lent by MISS FALCONER.

FRANZ HALS, 1584–1666.

136. Head of Woman. N.
Lent by WM. M. CHASE, ESQ.

E. S. HAMILTON.

137. Miss S. N.
Lent by E. S. HAMILTON, ESQ.

ROBERT GORDON HARDIE.

138. Lady. E.
Lent by R. G. HARDIE, ESQ.

139. Lady. S.
Lent by R. G. HARDIE, ESQ.

CHESTER HARDING, 1792–1866.

140. Mrs. Jas. S. Mitchell, *née* Miss Rebecca B. Coburn. E.
Lent by MRS. LAURENCE HUTTON.

SIR GEORGE HAYTER, 1792-1871.

141. Mrs. Ann Heylyn.   N.
Lent by EDWARD HEYLYN, Esq.

142. Mrs. Harriet Heylyn.   N.
Lent by EDWARD HEYLYN, Esq.

PROF. HUBERT HERKOMER, R.A.

143. Miss Jeannie Jewett Williams.   S.
Lent by CHAS. H. WILLIAMS, Esq.

ROSWELL S. HILL.

144. Portrait Study.   S.
Lent by ROSWELL S. HILL, Esq.

ROBERT HINCKLEY.

145. Mrs. Hinckley.   E.
Lent by ROBERT HINCKLEY, Esq.

R. HINTON-PERRY.

146. Dr. Emilie Blackwell.   S.
Lent by DR. E. M. CUSHIER.

147. Mrs. Ione H. Perry.   W.
Lent by R. HINTON-PERRY, Esq.

WILLIAM HOGARTH, 1697–1764.

148. Â Man.   N.

    Lent by P. S. AVERY Esq.

FRANK HOLL.

149. C. L.   C.

    Lent by CHARLES LANIER, Esq.

150. C. V.   C.

    Lent by CORNELIUS VANDERBILT, Esq.

JOHN HOPPNER, 1758–1810.

151. Percy B. Shelley, the Poet, age 14.   N.

    Lent by HENRY G. MARQUAND, Esq.

THOMAS HUDSON (attributed to) 1701–1779.

152. Mary Ball, Mother of George Washington. N.

    Lent by EDWARD L. MORSE, Esq.

EDWARD HUGHES.

153. Mrs. Wm. Rhinelander Stewart.   C.

    Lent by WM. RHINELANDER STEWART, Esq.

GEORGE HUGHES.

154. Miss Julia Schwartz.   C.

         Lent by Mrs. J. SCHWARTZ.

DANIEL HUNTINGTON.

155. Edward Lauterbach.   S.

         Lent by EDWARD LAUTERBACH, Esq.

156. Bishop Potter.   S.

         Lent by Mrs. H. C. POTTER.

157. "My Cousin in Blue" (Portrait of Miss Wells).   W.

         Lent by Miss WELLS.

158. Lady.   W.

         Lent by Mrs. COLUMBUS ISELIN.

159. Mrs. Charles C. Dodge.   S.

         Lent by Gen. CHARLES C. DODGE.

160. Richard Grant White.   W.

         Lent by STANFORD WHITE, Esq.

161. Mrs. Richard Grant White.   W.

         Lent by STANFORD WHITE, Esq.

WILLIAM H. HYDE.

162. Miss Helen Potter.   C.
Lent by DR. ELIPHALET POTTER.

163. Miss Fannie.   W.
Lent by WM. H. HYDE, ESQ.

164. Miss Anna Lane.   S.
Lent by WM. H. HYDE, ESQ.

H. N. HYNEMAN.

165. Mrs. Eugene Clarke.   W.
Lent by EUGENE CLARKE, ESQ.

CHARLES CROMWELL INGHAM, 1796–1863.

166. Mrs. Thomas Bayly Cropper, *née* Rosina Mix, 1843.   N.
Lent by MISS CROPPER.

167. Mrs. Elisha Mix, *née* Elizabeth Burbidge, 1832.   C.
Lent by MISS CROPPER.

168. Miss Burbidge, 1849.   N.
Lent by MISS CROPPER.

SAMUEL ISHAM.

169. Lady.   C.

    Lent by SAMUEL ISHAM, Esq.

BENONI IRWIN.

170. Mrs. Charles N. Vilas.   W.

    Lent by CHARLES N. VILAS, Esq.

JACOBIDES.

171. Virginia and Perry.   S.

    Lent by Mrs. H. FAIRFIELD OSBORN.

JEAN GUSTAVE JACQUET.

172. Portrait.   E.

    Lent by H. C. FAHNESTOCK, Esq.

PHŒBE JENKS.

173. Daniel Chauncey, 2d.   W.

    Lent by DANIEL CHAUNCEY, Jr., Esq.

PAUL JOBERT.

174. Mrs. Paul Jobert.   C.

    Lent by PAUL JOBERT, Esq.

EASTMAN JOHNSON.

175. Mrs. Spencer Trask. E.
Lent by SPENCER TRASK, Esq.

176. Edwin Booth. S.
Lent by Mrs. EDWINA BOOTH GROSSMAN.

177. Mary Devlin, First Wife of Edwin Booth. S.
Lent by Mrs. EDWINA BOOTH GROSSMAN.

178. Portrait. S.
Lent by ARCHIBALD ROGERS, Esq.

179. Mrs. Frank Lawrence and Lady Vernon. E.
Lent by EASTMAN JOHNSON, Esq.

180. Mrs. Seligman. E.
Lent by Mr. D. L. EINSTEIN.

181. Master Sampson. W.
Lent by Mrs. E. POPE SAMPSON.

DORA WHEELER KEITH.

182. Laurence Hutton. E.
Lent by BOUDINOT KEITH, Esq.

SUSAN M. KETCHAM.

183. Lady. S.

    Lent by Miss S. M. KETCHAM.

G. H. KITCHEL.

184. Miss L. C.

    Lent by G. H. KITCHEL, Esq.

FRANK KOPPS.

185. Oliver H. Jones. W.

    Lent by Mrs. WALTON OAKLEY.

186. Walton Livingston Oakley. C.

    Lent by Mrs. WALTON OAKLEY.

JOHN LA FARGE.

187. "Boy and Dog" (Richard Hunt). S.

    Lent by ALBERT STICKNEY, Esq.

NICHOLAS BERNARD LAPICIE, 1745–1784.

188. Young Girl. N.

    Lent by GEORGE A. HEARN, Esq.

NICOLAS L'ARGILLIERE, 1656-1746.

189. A Lady.   N.
       Lent by GEORGE A. HEARN, ESQ.

SIR THOMAS LAWRENCE, P.R.A., 1769-1830.

190. Miss Anderson.   N.
       Lent by D. F. APPLETON, ESQ.

191. Miss Barron.   N.
       Lent by GEORGE A. HEARN, ESQ.

192. Lady Burdett.   N.
       Lent by T. J. BLAKESLEE, ESQ.

193. A Lady.   N.
       Lent by DR. F. H. BOSWORTH.

194. Child.   N.
       Lent by STANFORD WHITE, ESQ.

OLIVER T. LAY, 1845-1890.

195. Edwin Booth.   S.
       Lent by WILLIAM BISPHAM, ESQ.

SIR PETER LELY, 1617–1680.

196. Lady Falconberg (daughter of Oliver Cromwell.)   N.
Lent by EDWARD BRANDUS, Esq.

197. Duchess of Portsmouth.   N.
Lent by Miss WILKES.

198. Duchess of Cleveland.   N.
Lent by Miss WILKES.

LOUIS LOEB.

199. Mrs. B. Lande.   W.
Lent by B. LANDE, Esq.

JENNIE S. LOOP.

200. Mrs. Adam Tredwell Sackett.   W.
Lent by Mrs. A. T. SACKETT.

ALBERT LYNCH.

201. Miss Marjorie Gould.   S.
Lent by GEORGE JAY GOULD, Esq.

JOHN A. MAC DOUGALL.

202. Head.   W.
Lent by MRS. W. S. MACY.

JULES MACHARD.

203. Mrs. Levi P. Morton and her Children.   C.
Lent by HON. LEVI P. MORTON.

FREDERICK MAC MONNIES.

204. Plaster Models, Washington and Groups for the Memorial Arch, Washington
205. Square, New York.
Lent by FRED. MAC MONNIES, ESQ.

DON RAIMUNDO DE MADRAZO.

206. S. P. Avery.   S.
Painted in one sitting.
Lent by S. P. AVERY, ESQ.

207. John J. Emery.   S.
Lent by JOHN J. EMERY. ESQ.

EDOUARD MANET, 1833-1883.

208. A Lady.   C.
Lent by MISS MARY H. HEARN.

G. MARSIGLIA.

209. Portrait of Himself. N.
Lent by MRS. HERMAN BAETJER.

CONSTANT MAYER.

210. Baroness V. de Bellfort. S.
Lent by ALFRED L. JAROS, ESQ.

ANTOINE RAPHAEL MENGS, 1728–1779.

211. Portrait of Himself. N.
Lent by GEORGE A. HEARN, ESQ.

ANNA LEA MERRITT.

212. Children of W. Bayard Cutting. E.
Lent by WM. BAYARD CUTTING, ESQ.

STANLEY MIDDLETON.

213. Mrs. Henry Prentice. S.
Lent by MRS. HENRY PRENTICE.

214. Miss C. Martin. W.
Lent by MISS C. MARTIN.

PIERRE MIGNARD, 1612-1695.

215. Mlle. de Valois.   N.
   Lent by EDWARD BRANDUS, Esq.

216. Duc de Burgogne.   N.
   Lent by J. R. SUTTON, Esq.

OSCAR MILLER.

217. Miss Kendal.
   Lent by OSCAR MILLER, Esq.

FRANK D. MILLET.

218. Child.   C.
   Lent by Dr. GORHAM BACON.

219. Mrs. Francis Vinton Greene.   W.
   Lent by F. V. GREENE, Esq.

E. L. MORSE.

220. Miss Griswold.   C.
   Lent by E. L. MORSE, Esq.

A. MULLER-URY.

221. Mrs. Wm. F. King.   W.
   Lent by WILLIAM F. KING, Esq.

222. Chauncey M. Depew.   C.
   Lent by CHAUNCEY M. DEPEW, Esq.

223. Miss Mildred Gibert Townsend.   W.
   Lent by JAMES BLISS TOWNSEND, Esq.

E. MUNIER.

224. Emma P. Avery.   S.
   Lent by S. P. AVERY, Esq.

GEORGE C. MUNZIG.

225. Miss Edith C. Candee.   S.
   Lent by Mrs. CANDEE.

226. Miss Ruth Twombly.   W.
   Lent by HAMILTON McK. TWOMBLY, Esq.

227. Master Charles Lanier.   C.
   Lent by CHAS. LANIER, Esq.

228. Miss Mary Mildred Williams.   E.
   Lent by Mrs. WILLIAM BISLAND WILLIAMS.

CHARLES FREDERICK NAEGELE.

229. Mrs. Charles Frederick Naegele.   C.

Lent by C. F. NAEGELE, Esq.

230. Mrs. William Woodward, Jr.   S

Lent by Mrs. WM. WOODWARD, Jr.

CASPER NETSCHER, 1639-1684.

231. Henriette d'Angleterre.   N.

Lent by EDWARD BRANDUS, Esq.

RHODA HOLMES NICHOLS.

232. Mrs. Samuel Sloan, Jr.   W.

Lent by Mrs. SAMUEL SLOAN.

233. Mrs. Theodore Sutro.   C.

Lent by Mrs. THEODORE SUTRO.

234. Mme. C.   W.

Lent by Mrs. RHODA HOLMES NICHOLS.

KATE ROGERS NOWELL.

235. Miss D. R.   W.

Lent by Mrs. M. K. ROGERS.

WILLIAM PAGE, 1811–1885.

236. Mrs. Thaddeus Sherman.   W.

Lent by MRS. F. M. SCOTT.

CHARLES WILSON PEALE, 1741–1827.

237. General John Cropper, 1793.   N.

Lent by JOHN CROPPER, ESQ.

238. Mrs. John Cropper, 1792, *née* Catherine Bayley.   N.

Lent by JOHN CROPPER, ESQ.

REMBRANDT PEALE, 1787–1860.

239. George Washington.   C.

Lent by MISS CAROLINE PHELPS STOKES.

240. Martha Washington.   C.

Lent by MISS CAROLINE PHELPS STOKES.

ELLA F. PELL.

241. Miss Mackaye.   W.

Lent by J. SCOTT HARTLEY, ESQ.

HARPER PENNINGTON.

242. Portrait. C.

  Lent by REGINALD DE KOVEN, Esq.

243. Children of Wm. Rhinelander Stewart. E.

  Lent by WM. RHINELANDER STEWART, Esq.

E. WOOD PERRY, Jr.

244. Gen. Grant. W.

  Painted in San Francisco, 1879.

  Lent by E. WOOD PERRY, Jr., Esq.

BENJAMIN CURTIS PORTER.

245. Miss Edith Shepard. S.

  Lent by Mrs. ELLIOTT F. SHEPARD.

246. "Le Soir." Portrait of Mrs. W. Jay Schieffelin. S.

  Lent by Mrs. ELLIOTT F. SHEPARD.

247. Miss Lila V. Sloane. S.

  Lent by WM. D. SLOANE, Esq.

248. Mrs. Wm. C. Schermerhorn. E.

  Lent by WM. C. SCHERMERHORN, Esq.

249. Master Sidney Porter. S.
Lent by MRS. BENJAMIN C. PORTER.

250. Mrs. H. P. King. W.
Lent by MRS. M. D. SPAULDING.

ROBERT REID.

251. Portrait. W.
Lent by ROBERT REID, ESQ.

SIR JOSHUA REYNOLDS, 1732–1792.

252. Lady. N.
Lent by D. F. APPLETON, ESQ.

253. Hon. Mrs. Stanhope. N.
Lent by HENRY G. MARQUAND, ESQ.

WM. M. J. RICE.

254. Portrait. S.
Lent by E. C. HENDERSON, ESQ.

255. Lady. W.
Lent by J. S. CRANE, ESQ.

GASPARD RIGAUD, 1659–1743.

256. Louis XIV.   N.
Lent by EDWARD BRANDUS, Esq.

LUCIE LEE ROBBINS.

257. Lucie Lee Robbins.   S.
Lent by Mrs. THATCHER M. ADAMS.

GEORGE ROMNEY, 1734–1802.

258. Elizabeth Carter.   N.
Lent by EDWARD HEYLYN, Esq.

259. "The Shy Girl."   N.
Lent by HENRY G. MARQUAND, Esq.

260. Lady Gordon.   N.
Lent by GEORGE A. HEARN, Esq.

261. Lady Hamilton.   N.
Lent by T. KIRKPATRICK, Esq.

262. Lady.   N.
Lent by STANFORD WHITE, Esq.

THOMAS P. ROSSITER, 1817–1871.

263. Mrs. Rogers Hoffman.   C.
    Lent by Mrs. GEO. HOFFMAN.

SAMUEL W. ROWSE.

264. Josephine.   S.
    Lent by Mrs. H. FAIRFIELD OSBORN.

PETER PAUL RUBENS, 1577–1640.

265. Head of Boy.   N.
    Lent by WM. M. CHASE, Esq.

JOHN RUSSELL, R.A. 1745–1806.

266. Lady.   N.
    Lent by GEORGE A. HEARN, Esq.

JOHN S. SARGENT.

267. Beatrice.   S.
    Lent by Mrs. ROBERT GOELET.

268. Child.   W.
    Lent by Dr. GORHAM BACON.

269. Portrait. · S.
   Lent by JACOB WENDELL, Esq.

270. Miss Helen Dunham. E.
   Lent by JAMES H. DUNHAM, Esq.

271. Miss Ada Rehan. S.
   Lent by Mrs. G. M. WHITIN.

SARAH C. SEARS.

272. Miss Ruth Simpkins. S.
   Lent by J. M. SEARS, Esq.

JOSEPH SEVERN.

273. John Keats, The Poet. N.
   Lent by Mrs. J. G. SPEED.

274. George Keats. N.
   Lent by Mrs. J. G. SPEED.

275. Tom Keats. N.
   Lent by Mrs. J. G. SPEED.

AMANDA BREWSTER SEWELL.

276. Mrs. Loring Brace. W.
   Lent by LORING BRACE, Esq.

277. Mrs. Boudinot Keith. C.
   Lent by Mrs. CANDACE WHEELER.

J. J. SHANNON.

278. Mrs. James Creelman. S.

    Lent by JAMES CREELMAN, Esq.

J. SHARPLESS, 1746–1813.

279. Robert R. Livingston, Chancellor of State of N. Y., 1777–1801, Administered the Oath of Office to Washington at his First Inauguration. N.

    Lent by MRS. ALFRED NELSON.

280. Alexander Hamilton. N.

    Lent by the MISSES HAMILTON.

WILLIAM OLIVER STONE, 1830–1875.

281. Portrait. S.

    Lent by MRS. CANDACE WHEELER.

C. HOBART STICKLAND.

282. Mrs. Alfred Hennen Morris. E.

    Lent by MRS. A. H. MORRIS.

283. Miss Martha Strickland. S.

    Lent by MRS. J. W. A. STRICKLAND.

GILBERT STUART, 1755–1828.

284. Hon. Edward Everett.   N.
      Lent by MRS. J. W. MILLER.

285. Portrait (Unfinished Study).   N.
      Lent by S. P. AVERY, ESQ.

286. George Washington.   N.
      Lent by D. F. APPLETON, ESQ.

287. Daniel D. Rogers.   N.
      Lent by JOHN ROGERS, ESQ.

288. George Bethune.   N.
      Lent by FANEUIL D. WEISSE, M.D.

289. Gouverneur Kemble.   N.
      Lent by MRS. HENRY A. SIMONDS.

290. Peter Kemble.   N.
      Lent by MRS. HENRY A. SIMONDS.

291. John Callender.   N.
      Lent by MISS MARY R. CALLENDER.

292. George Washington.   N.
      Lent by CHAUNCEY M. DEPEW, ESQ.

THOMAS SULLY, 1783–1872.

293. Mrs. George Hoffman.   N.
      Lent by MRS. GEORGE HOFFMAN.

294. Mrs. James Fairlie.   N.
Lent by MRS. ALFRED NELSON.

295. Dr. William Potts Dewees.   N.
Lent by MRS. H. M. DEWEES.

296. Mrs. Stacy B. Bispham.   N.
Lent by WILLIAM BISPHAM, ESQ.

297. Wm. Royal Johnston.   N.
Lent by STILSON HUTCHINS.

298. Mrs. I. R. Jackson and Mrs. John Lee.   N.
Lent by MRS. OSWALD JACKSON.

299. Mrs. Richard H. Bayard.   N.
Lent by MRS. OSWALD JACKSON.

300. Mrs. I. R. Jackson.   N.
Lent by MRS. OSWALD JACKSON.

JUSTUS SUSTERMANS, 1597–1681.

301. Orazio Piccolomini of Siena.   N.
Lent by R. FULTON CUTTING, ESQ.

JOSÉ TAPIRÒ.

302. Fatma, wife of the Jailor of Tangier, Morocco.   N.
Lent by MRS. RICHARD A. McCURDY.

EDMUND C. TARBELL.

303. "My Sister Lydia."   E.
Lent by BENJAMIN HATCH, Esq.

ABBOTT H. THAYER.

304. Portrait.   S.
Lent by JOSHUA M. SEARS, Esq.

WILLIAM THORNE.

305. Miss M. B.   W.
Lent by HENRY ALEXANDER MURRAY, Esq.

306. Portrait.   W.
Lent by Mrs. OAKLEIGH THORN.

307. Portrait.   S.
Lent by DALLAS B. PRATT, Esq.

308. Portrait.   S.
Lent by DALLAS B. PRATT, Esq.

309. John D. Wing.   C.
Lent by Mrs. JOHN D. WING.

V. TOJETTI.

310. Miss Florence Lauterbach.   C.
Lent by EDW. LAUTERBACH, Esq.

JOHN TRUMBULL, 1756-1843.

311. Frances Platt Townsend Lupton.
Lent by MRS. W. CUMMINGS STORY,

C. Y. TURNER.

312. Major-General Josiah Porter.   W.
Lent by MISS MARY PORTER.

DIRK VAN DALEN, c. 1623-1665.

313. Dutch Lady.   N.
Lent by T. J. BLAKESLEE, ESQ.

BARTHOLOMEW VAN DER HELST, 1613-1670.

314. Princesse d'Orange.   N.
Lent by EDWARD BRANDUS, ESQ.

MARY VAN DER VEER.

315. Miss V. V.   W.
Lent by MISS MARY VAN DER VEER.

JACQUES VAN LOO, 1684-1745.

316. Duc de Bassompierre.   N.
Lent by EDWARD BRANDUS, ESQ.

317. Man. N.
Lent by GEORGE A. HEARN, Esq.

THEODORE VAN THULDEN, 1606–1676.

318. Isabella Brandt. N.
Lent by GEORGE A. HEARN, Esq.

PIETER VERELST, 1614–1668.

319. Man. N.
Lent by WILLIAM MACBETH, Esq.

HECTOR VIGER, 1819–1879.

320. Queen Hortense. N.
Lent by EDWARD BRANDUS, Esq.

CLARA VOLKMAN.

321. Daughter of Count Schlippenbach-Schönermarck. S.
Lent by COUNT SCHLIPPENBACH-SCHÖNERMARCK.

GEORGE B. WALDO.

322. Miss Margaret Dunn. C.
Lent by GEORGE B. WALDO, Esq.

SAMUEL WALDO, 1783-1861.

323. John Nelson Lloyd (painted in collaboration with Wm. S. Jewett). N.
 Lent by CHARLOTTE LLOYD SCHMIDT.

HENRY OLIVER WALKER.

324. Mrs. Wm. T. Evans and her Son. E.
 Lent by WM. T. EVANS, Esq.

J. HANSON WALKER.

325. Fairfield. W.
 Lent by MRS. H. FAIRFIELD OSBORN.

J. ALDEN WEIR.

326. Portraits of two Sisters. S.
 Lent by J. ALDEN WEIR, Esq.

327. Richard Grant White. W.
 Lent by STANFORD WHITE, Esq.

BENJAMIN WEST, P.R.A., 1738-1820.

328. Robert Fulton. N.
 Lent by R. FULTON CUTTING, Esq.

JAMES McNEIL WHISTLER.

329. Portrait Study.   W.
       Lent by E. G. KENNEDY, Esq.

SARAH W. WHITMAN.

330. Portrait.   W.
       Lent by Rev. D. MERRIMAN.

331. Boy.   C.
       Lent by F. H. PRINCE, Esq.

M. U. WHITLOCK.

332. Miss Cecilia Beaux.   C.
       Lent by Miss WHITLOCK.

WM. J. WHITTEMORE.

333. Miss W.   E.
       Lent by WM. J. WHITTEMORE, Esq.

334. Little Miss S.   S.
       Lent by Miss SLOANE.

IRVING R. WILES.

335. Miss Gladys W.   C.
       Lent by IRVING R. WILES, Esq.

J. H. WITT.

336. Mrs. Rosa Sutro.   S.

       Lent by THEODORE SUTRO, Esq.

337. Miss J.   C.

       Lent by J. H. WITT, Esq.

338. Miss H.   S.

       Lent by J. H. WITT, Esq.

ZORN.

339. George H. Bend.   S.

       Lent by Mrs. GEORGE H. BEND.

340. T. M. Wheeler.   S.

       Lent by Mrs. CANDACE WHEELER.

UNKNOWN.

341. Harriet Duer Robinson.

       Lent by Mrs. H. D. ROBINSON.

342. Henrietta Maria, Queen of Charles First of England.   N.

       Lent by ALEXANDER W. DRAKE, Esq.

343. Francis I. of France.   N.

       Lent by ALEXANDER W. DRAKE, Esq.

344. Girl, Spanish School. N.
Lent by ALEXANDER W. DRAKE, Esq.

345. Robert Fulton. N.
Lent by WM. BAYARD CUTTING, Esq.

346. Miss Betty Richardson. N.
Lent by JAMES W. GERARD, Esq.

347. Shute Shrimpton Yeamans (1721-1769). N.
Lent by JAMES W. GERARD, Esq.

348. Sarah Jennings, Duchess of Marlborough. N.
Lent by Miss CROPPER.

349. Portrait. N.
Lent by WM. M. CHASE, Esq.

350. Philip IV. of Spain. N.
Lent by WM. M. CHASE, Esq.

351. Lucy Sinclair, wife of Gordon Sage, aged 17 (1797). E.
Lent by DOROTHY SINCLAIR RENNARD.

MINIATURES.

AUBRY.

352. Rosalie Duthé.
Lent by EDWARD BRANDUS, Esq.

353. Mlle. de la Jadelière.
Lent by EDWARD BRANDUS, Esq.

AUGUSTIN.

354. Mlle. de Beaucourt (1789).
Lent by EDWARD BRANDUS, Esq.

355. Lady of the First Empire.
Lent by EDWARD BRANDUS, Esq.

WILLIAM J. BAER.

356. The Golden Hour.
Lent by A. C. C., Esq.

357. Mrs. C. H. L., Jr.
Lent by C. H. L., Jr., Esq.

358. Good Friends.

Lent by T. L. P., Esq.

359. My First-Born.

Lent by J. BAER, Esq.

BAUZIL.

360. Louis du Mont (1791).

Lent by EDWARD BRANDUS, Esq.

Mrs. K. A. BEHENNA.

361. Miss G.

Lent by Mrs. BEHENNA.

362. Miss Mabel R.

Lent by Mrs. BEHENNA.

363. Miss Knowlton.

Lent by PETER MARIÉ, Esq.

364. Mrs. L. Wilmerding.

Lent by PETER MARIÉ, Esq.

365. Princess Brancaccio.

Lent by PETER MARIÉ, Esq.

366. Miss Dexter.

Lent by PETER MARIÉ, Esq.

367. Mrs. Isaac Bell.
Lent by PETER MARIÉ, Esq.

368. Mrs. Griswold.
Lent by PETER MARIÉ, Esq.

369. Miss Brewster.
Lent by PETER MARIÉ, Esq.

370. Child.
Lent by Mrs. K. A. BEHENNA.

371. Miss Vivian Behenna.
Lent by Mrs. K. A. BEHENNA.

372. Miss Vivian Behenna.
Lent by Mrs. K. A. BEHENNA.

373. Peter Marié.
Lent by PETER MARIÉ, Esq.

374. Italian Peasant.
Lent by PETER MARIÉ, Esq.

375. Portrait Study, Marie M.
Lent by PETER MARIÉ, Esq.

376. Miss M. Renwee.
Lent by Mrs. K. A. BEHENNA.

377. Portrait Study, Marie M.
Lent by Mrs. K. A. BEHENNA.

378. Child.
Lent by Mrs. K. A. BEHENNA.

379. J. H. Twachtman.
Lent by Mrs. K. A. BEHENNA.

380. Portrait Study, French Model.
Lent by Mrs. K. A. BEHENNA.

381. Miss W. (Unfinished.)
Lent by Mrs. K. A. BEHENNA.

382. Italian Model.
Lent by Mrs. K. A. BEHENNA.

383. Mrs. Potter Palmer.
Lent by Mrs. K. A. BEHENNA.

384. Baby.
Lent by Mrs. K. A. BEHENNA.

385. Mlle. Marcelle.
Lent by Mrs. K. A. BEHENNA.

GEORGE BONAWITZ.

386. Mr. A.
Lent by J. A., Esq.

BOSSET (attributed to).

387. Princesse de Croy.

    Lent by EDWARD BRANDUS, Esq.

CAMPANA.

388. Mme. Polignac.

    Lent by EDWARD BRANDUS, Esq.

GEORGINE CAMPBELL.

389. Mrs. B. Thaw.

    Lent by B. THAW, Esq.

390. Portrait.

    Lent by B. THAW, Esq.

391. Son of J. Hooker Hamersley, Esq.

    Lent by Mrs. J. HOOKER HAMERSLEY.

392. Mrs. James B. Eades.

    Lent by Mrs. EADES HAZARD.

393. Mrs. Francis P. Freeman.

    Lent by FRANCIS P. FREEMAN, Esq.

394. Mrs. Charles Sprague.

    Lent by CHAS. SPRAGUE, Esq.

395. Katharine Drexel Penrose.
Lent by Dr. PENROSE.

396. Daughter of J. Hooker Hamersley. Esq.
Lent by Mrs. J. HOOKER HAMERSLEY.

397. Miss. F. Lurman.
Lent by Mrs. J. HOOKER HAMERSLEY.

398. Dr. Wm. Argyle Watson.
Lent by Dr. WM. ARGYLE WATSON.

399. Portrait.
Lent by Dr. WM. ARGYLE WATSON.

400. Son of Fitzhugh Whitehouse, Esq.
Lent by Dr. WM. ARGYLE WATSON.

401. Francis P. Freeman.
Lent by Mrs. FRANCIS P. FREEMAN.

CARBILLET.

402. Marquise de Crequy.
Lent by EDWARD BRANDUS, Esq.

JOHN CARLIN.

403. Portrait.
Lent by Mrs. JOHN CARLIN.

404. Portrait.
>   *Lent by* MRS. JOHN CARLIN.

405. Portrait.
>   *Lent by* MRS. JOHN CARLIN.

406. Portrait.
>   *Lent by* MRS. JOHN CARLIN.

FRANCES S. CARLIN.

407. Portrait.
>   *Lent by* FRANCES S. CARLIN.

408. Portrait.
>   *Lent by* FRANCES S. CARLIN.

409. Portrait.
>   *Lent by* FRANCES S. CARLIN.

410. Portrait.
>   *Lent by* FRANCES S. CARLIN.

411. Portrait.
>   *Lent by* MRS. THOS. H. BARBER.

412. Portrait.
>   *Lent by* MISS S.

413. Portrait.
>   *Lent by* D. PARKS FACKLER, ESQ.

CHARLES J. CHAPLIN.

414. Portrait.

    Lent by STANFORD WHITE, Esq.

GEORGE RENLING COLE.

415. Mrs. Alexander N. Fullerton.

    Lent by Mrs. ALEX. N. FULLERTON.

AGNES COLES.

416. Miss Ethel Rockefeller.

    Lent by Mrs. WM. ROCKEFELLER.

417. Wm. P. Coles.

    Lent by THEODORE P. JENKINS, Esq.

418. J. S. T. Stranahan.

    Lent by Miss AGNES COLES.

419. Gretchen Walradt.

    Lent by Miss AGNES COLES.

420. Kathleen Jenkins.

    Lent by Mrs. THEODORE. P. JENKINS.

421. Rachel.

    Lent by Mrs. M. K. BATES.

422. Mrs. Howard Jones.
>Lent by Miss AGNES COLES.

COSWAY (attributed to).

423. Lady of the First Empire.
>Lent by EDWARD BRANDUS, Esq.

H. DARBY.

424. The Thieves.
>Lent by Mrs. V. D. VER PLANCK.

DAVID.

425. Marie Sallée (Danseuse).
>Lent by EDWARD BRANDUS, Esq.

ISABELLE DAVIS.

426. Miss E. E. Davis.
>Lent by Miss ISABELLE DAVIS.

427. Young Girl.
>Lent by Miss ISABELLE DAVIS.

428. Mrs. J. J. Davis.
>Lent by Miss ISABELLE DAVIS.

429. Lady.
>Lent by Miss ISABELLE DAVIS.

M. DAYTON.

430. Master McKee.
      Lent by GEN. BENJAMIN HARRISON.

431. Baby's Head.
      Lent by M. DAYTON, ESQ.

432. Mrs. Gertrude V. C. Hamilton, Jr.
      Lent by MRS. G. V. C. HAMILTON, JR.

433. Portrait Study.
      Lent by M. DAYTON, ESQ.

434. Miss McKee.
      Lent by GEN. BENJAMIN HARRISON.

435. Violet Hamilton.
      Lent by MRS. G. V. C. HAMILTON, JR.

436. Dutch Girl.
      Lent by M. DAYTON, ESQ.

437. Miss Susie Tucker.
      Lent by MRS. W. H. JOHNSTON.

MME. GREGORIO DE AJURIA.

438. Oria de Ajuria.
      Lent by MME. GREGORIO DE AJURIA.

439. Miss Kate Brice.
Lent by MRS. CALVIN S. BRICE.

440. Mrs. Eben Sumner Draper.
Lent by MRS. EBEN SUMNER DRAPER.

441. President Felix Faure.
Lent by PRESIDENT FAURE.

442. Caroll Harriman.
Lent by MRS. E. H. HARRIMAN.

DE BEAUFORT.

443. Loius XV.
Lent by EDWARD BRANDUS, ESQ.

J. J. DE TERSET.

444. Mme. de Virien.
Lent by EDWARD BRANDUS, ESQ.

DEWINE.

445. Lady, Period of Louis XVI.
Lent by EDWARD BRANDUS, ESQ.

DUMONT.

446. Lady, 1787.
Lent by EDWARD BRANDUS, ESQ.

MARY E. ELMER.

447. Mrs. William P. Douglas.
Lent by MARY F. ELMER.

448. Mrs. Walter Stanton.
Lent by MRS. WALTER STANTON.

449. Mrs. I. O. Rhines.
Lent by MRS. I. O. RHINES.

450. Mrs. Edwin H. Blashfield.
Lent by MRS. E. H. BLASHFIELD.

451. Mrs. William Douglas.
Lent by MRS. I. O. RHINES.

452. Henry G. Marquand.
Lent by H. MARY F. ELMER.

453. General Darr.
Lent by F. DARR, ESQ.

454. Mr. Frank J. A. Darr.
Lent by F. DARR, ESQ.

T. FERRI.

455. Empress Josephine.
Lent by EDWARD BRANDUS, ESQ.

MISS HALE.

456. Anne Bard, wife of Edward Prime.

Lent by EDWARD PRIME, Esq.

ANNE S. HOBBS.

457. Mrs. A. R.

Lent by Mrs. ANDREW ROBESON.

INMAN.

458. Mrs. Alexander Hamilton.

Lent by THE MISSES HAMILTON.

R. KEELING.

459. Mrs. Burke Roche.

Lent by R. KEELING, Esq.

460. Mrs. James Brown Potter.

Lent by R. KEELING, Esq.

LACROIX.

461. Lady, Period of Louis XVI.

Lent by EDWARD BRANDUS, Esq.

LAGRÉNÉE.

462. Gen. Napier.
    Lent by EDWARD BRANDUS, Esq.

LEDOUX.

463. Mlle. Maillart.
    Lent by EDWARD BRANDUS, Esq.

JOHN A. MacDOUGALL.

464. Mrs. Rebecca Morse.
    Lent by Mrs. MORSE.

465. Miss Jeanette Corse.
    Lent by Miss CORSE.

466. Elie.
    Lent by J. A. MacDOUGALL, Esq.

MISS FLORENCE MACKUBIN.

467. Mrs. Charles J. Bonaparte.
    Lent by C. J. BONAPARTE, Esq.

468. Mrs. Josias J. George.
    Lent by J. J. GEORGE, Esq.

469. Mrs. Edwin Stanton.
Lent by MRS. ELEANOR BUSH.

470. Mrs. E. Davis.
Lent by MRS. J. E. McGOWAN.

471. Mrs. George Wright.
Lent by MISS WRIGHT.

472. Mrs. George Curtis Snow.
Lent by MRS. GEORGE C. SNOW.

473. Miss Perkins.
Lent by MISS PERKINS.

474. Mrs. M. C. S.
Lent by MISS BENJAMIN.

475. Mrs. J. H. R. H.
Lent by MISS BENJAMIN.

MAJESKY.

476. Portrait.
Lent by MRS. ALFRED D. BRINK, JR.

MALBONE, 1803.

477. Mrs. Alexander Bleeker.
Lent by CHARLES M. LEA, ESQ.

MARX.

478. Maria Livingston, wife of Commodore
J. C. Stevens.
Lent by ROBT. CAMBRIDGE LIVINGSTON, Esq.

MATHIEU-DEROCHE.

479. F. C. Havemeyer.
Lent by Mrs. F. W. JACKSON.

MAURUS.

480. Mrs. Victoria W. Graham and Children.
Lent by CHAS. DOUGLAS GRAHAM, Esq.

MIGNARD.

481. Mlle. de Fontanes.
Lent by EDWARD BRANDUS, Esq.

HUGH NICHOLSON.

482. Mrs. David C. Townsend.
Lent by DAVID C. TOWNSEND, Esq.

NOLLE.

483. Empress Marie Louise.
Lent by EDWARD BRANDUS, Esq.

ALVA PEARSALL.

484. Master Charles Pratt.
Lent by MRS. F. B. PRATT.

485. Alva Pearsall.
Lent by MRS. M. M. PEARSALL.

486. Mrs. Wilmerding.
Lent by ALVA PEARSALL.

MRS. C. E. PENNOYER.

487. Lady.
Lent by THEODORE B. STARR, ESQ.

488. "Stella."
Lent by THEODORE B. STARR, ESQ.

489. Duchess of Leinster.
Lent by THEODORE B. STARR, ESQ.

490. Head, after Cosway.
Lent by THEODORE B. STARR, ESQ.

LILA POLLOCK.

491. Mrs. Rosa Brown Crichton.
Lent by REV. JOHN W. BROWN.

PRUD'HON.

492. Lady, Period First Empire.
>   *Lent by* EDWARD BRANDUS, Esq.

J. STAPLES ROWE.

493. William MacNeill Rodewald.
>   *Lent by* WM. MacNEILL RODEWALD, Esq.

494. Mrs. William MacNeill Rodewald.
>   *Lent by* WM. MacNEILL RODEWALD, Esq.

495. Mrs. Chas. Frederick Hoffman, Jr.
>   *Lent by* C. F. HOFFMAN, Jr., Esq.

496. Mrs. Edward Courtland Gale.
>   *Lent by* EDW. C. GALE, Esq.

497. Baby Caritte.
>   *Lent by* J. STAPLES ROWE, Esq.

498. Mrs. Joseph Stickney.
>   *Lent by* JOSEPH STICKNEY, Esq.

499. Robert Tailer.
>   *Lent by* MRS. ROBT. W. TAILER.

500. Mrs. Julia W. Hirsch.
>   *Lent by* J. STAPLES ROWE, Esq.

501. Jesse Seligman.
>Lent by MRS. E. WASSERMANN.

502. Mrs. Jerome Hurlburt.
>Lent by MRS. ALFRED RAY.

ROZE.

503. Mme. Vermont, 1792.
>Lent by EDWARD BRANDUS, ESQ.

SINGRY.

504. Emperor Napoleon I.
>Lent by EDWARD BRANDUS, ESQ.

EMILY DRAYTON TAYLOR.

505. Mrs. Henry C. Lea.
>Lent by CHARLES M. LEA.

506. Miss Sturgis.
>Lent by MRS. J. MADISON TAYLOR.

507. John Drayton.
>Lent by MRS. J. MADISON TAYLOR.

508. Mrs. S. Weir Mitchell.
>Lent by MRS. S. WEIR MITCHELL.

509. Miss Maria G. Mitchell.
>   *Lent by* MRS. S. WEIR MITCHELL.

510. Dr. S. Weir Mitchell.
>   *Lent by* MRS. S. WEIR MITCHELL.

511. Miss Anna B. Newbold.
>   *Lent by* MISS ANNA B. NEWBOLD.

512. Mabel Heyward Taylor.
>   *Lent by* MRS. J. MADISON TAYLOR.

VAN LOO.

513. Marquise de Poyanne, 1756.
>   *Lent by* EDWARD BRANDUS, ESQ.

VILLERS.

514. Mlle. Elisa de Tilly, 1807.
>   *Lent by* EDWARD BRANDUS, ESQ.

ETHEL WEBLING.

515. Miss Betty.
>   *Lent by* ETHEL WEBLING.

516. An English Girl.
>   *Lent by* ETHEL WEBLING.

517. Miss Agnes Garrett.
>*Lent by* ETHEL WEBLING.

518. Mrs. H. J. J. and Child.
>*Lent by* ETHEL WEBLING.

519. Edwin Booth as Hamlet.
>*Lent by* ETHEL WEBLING.

520. Miss L. Atkinson.
>*Lent by* ETHEL WEBLING.

521. Miss Lucy Webling.
>*Lent by* ETHEL WEBLING.

522. Mrs. Gerald Wellesley.
>*Lent by* ETHEL WEBLING.

523. John Ruskin.
>*Lent by* ETHEL WEBLING.

WEYLER.

524. Mlle. de Mirpoix, 1771.
>*Lent by* EDWARD BRANDUS, ESQ.

A. H. WOLFF.

525. Miss Aleid Schenck.
>*Lent by* MRS. J. FREDERICK SCHENCK.

UNKNOWN.

526. Junius-Brutus Booth, the Elder, father of Edwin Booth.
    Lent by MRS. EDWINA BOOTH GROSSMAN.

527. Evelina Van Vredenburgh, wife of Gov. Enos. T. Throop of New York.
    Lent by MRS. WM. CUMMINGS STORY.

528. Elizabeth Platt Townsend, wife of Col. Van Vredenburgh.
    Lent by MRS. CUMMINGS STORY.

529. Mrs. George C. Bacon of Kentucky.
    Lent by MRS. J. G. SPEED.

530. Judge Garrard of Kentucky.
    Lent by MRS. J. G. SPEED.

531. Mrs. Fred Earnest of Louisiana.
    Lent by MRS. J. G. SPEED.

532. Mrs. George C. Gwathmey of Kentucky.
    Lent by MRS. J. G. SPEED.

533. G. Marsiglia, 1817.
    Lent by WILLIAM MARSIGLIA NESBIT, ESQ.

534. Charles François Eugene Le Brun, 1795.
    Lent by NAPOLEON LE BRUN, ESQ.

535. Mrs. Victoria W. Graham.
Lent by CHAS. D. GRAHAM, Esq.

536. Czar Paul I. of Russia.
Lent by EDWARD BRANDUS, Esq.

537. Peter the Great.
Enamel.
Lent by EDWARD BRANDUS, Esq.

538. Lacazette and Mlle. Desbrosse.
Lent by EDWARD BRANDUS, Esq.

539. Mrs. Ann Heylyn, *née* Carter.
Lent by EDWARD HEYLYN, Esq.

540. Portrait after Greuze.
Enamel.
Lent by THOS. KIRKPATRICK, Esq.

INDEX OF SUBJECTS.

M. stands for Miniature.

Alexander, Mrs. Charles B., 130.
Alexander, James W., 3.
Alexander, James W., Jr., 5.
Anderson, Miss, 190.
Atkinson, Miss L., M.
Avery, Ellen Walters, 10.
Avery, Emma P., 224.
Avery, S. P., 114, 206.
Avery, Mrs. S. P., 9.
Ayer, Mrs. J. C. 110.

Bacon, Mrs. George C., M.
Ball, Mary—Mother of Geo. Washington, 152.
Barron, Miss, 191.
Bayard, Mrs. Richard H. 299.
Beardsley, Judge Levi, 6.
Beaux, Miss Cecilia, 332.
Behenna, Miss Vivian, M.
Bell, Mrs. Isaac, M.
Bend, George H., 339.
Bethune, George, 288.
Betty, Miss, M.
Bishop of Albany, 124.

Bispham, Mrs. Stacy B., 296.
Blackwell, Dr. Emilie, 146.
Blashfield, Mrs. Edwin H., M.
Bleeker, Mrs. Alexander, M.
Bonaparte, Mrs. Charles J., M.
Booth, Edwin, 176, 195, M.
Booth, Mary Devlin, 177.
Booth, Junius Brutus, M.
Brace, Mrs. Loring, 276.
Brancaccio, Princess, M.
Brandt, Isabella, 318.
Brewster, Miss, M.
Brice, Mrs. Calvin S., and Daughters, 111.
Brice, Miss Kate, M.
Bridgham, Mrs. Samuel W., 25.
Burbidge, Miss, 168.
Burdett, Lady, 192.

Callender, John, 291.
Calvé in " Carmen," 60.
Candee, Miss Edith C., 225.
Carl IV. of Bavaria, 99.
Carpenter, Dudley S., 33.
Carter, Elizabeth, 258.
Case, Meigs, M.D., 51.
Charles of France, 74.
Charlotte, Princess, 126.
Chase, Alice Dieudonnée, 65.
Chase, William M., 102.
Chauncey, Daniel, 2d, 173.
Chauncey, Mrs. Daniel, 26.
Clarke, Mrs. Eugene, 165.
Cleveland, Duchess of, 198.

Coles, Wm. P., M.
Corse, Miss Jeanette, M.
Cotton, Mrs. Leslie, 89.
Creelman, Mrs. James, 278.
Crichton, Mrs. Rosa Brown, M.
Cropper, Gen. John, 237.
Cropper, Mrs. John, 131.
Cropper, Mrs. John, 238.
Cropper, Mrs. Thomas Bayly, 166.
Cutting, R. Fulton, 29.
Cutting, William Bayard, 30.
Cutting, W. Bayard, Children of, 212.

D'Angleterre, Henriette, 231.
Darr, Mrs. Frank J. A., M.
Darr, Gen., M.
Davis, Mrs. E., M.
Davis, Miss E. E., M.
Davis, Mrs. J. J., M.
Davis, Mrs. J. W. A., 19.
de Ajuria, Oria, M.
de Bassompierre, Duc, 316.
de Beaucourt, Mlle., M.
de Bellfort, Baroness, V., 210.
de Burgogne, Duc, 216.
de Crequy, Marquise, M.
de Croy, Princesse, M.
de Fontanes, Mlle., M.
Delafield, Mrs. Edward, 8.
de la Jadeliere, Mlle., M.
de Llanos, Fanny Keats, 97.
de Louvois, Marquise, 100.
de Mirpoix, Mlle., M.

Depew, Chauncey M., 222.
de Polignac, Mme., M.
de Pompadour, Mme., 57.
de Poyanne, Marquise, M.
de Rham, Charles, 3d, 119.
de Tilly, Mlle. Elisa, M.
de Valois, Mlle., 215.
de Virien, Mme., M.
Dewees, Dr. William Potts, 295.
Dexter, Miss, M.
Dexter, Mrs. Newton, 23.
Dix, Rev. Morgan, D.D., 37.
Doane, Bishop, 124.
Dodge, Mrs. Charles C., 159.
d'Orange, Princesse, 314.
d'Orleans, Mme., 105.
Douglas, Mrs. Wm., M.
Douglas, Mrs. Wm. P., M.
Draper, Mrs. Eben Sumner, M.
Drayton, John, M.
Du Mont, Louis, M.
Duncan, Francis, 80.
Dunn, Miss Margaret, 322.
Dunham, Miss Helen, 270.
Duthe, Rosalie, M.

Eades, Mrs. James B., M.
Earnest, F., M.
Elie M.
Eliot, Josiah, 82.
Emery, John J., 207.
Evans, Mrs. Wm. T. and Son, 324.
Everett, Hon. Edward, 284.

Fairlie, Mrs. James, 294.
Falconberg, Lady, 196.
Fatma, 302.
Faure, President Felix, M.
Flower, Mrs. Anson R., 17.
Forbes, Norman, 122.
Forrest, Edwin, 116.
Francis I. of France, 343.
Freeman, Francis P., M.
Freeman, Mrs. Francis P., M.
Fullerton, Mrs. Alex. N., M.
Fulton, Robert, 328, 345.

Gale, Mrs. Edward Courtland, M.
Garrard, Judge, M.
Garrett, Miss Agnes, M.
George, Henry, 39.
George, Mrs. Josias J., M.
Goelet, Miss Beatrice, 267.
Gordon, Lady, 260.
Gould, Mrs. George J., 109.
Gould, Miss Marjorie, 201.
Graham, Mrs. Victoria W., and Children, M.
Grant, Gen., 244.
Greene, Mrs. Francis Vinton, 219.
Griswold, Miss, 220.
Griswold, Mrs., M.
Gwathmey, Mrs. George C., M.

Hamersley, J. Hooker, Daughter of, M.
Hamersley, J. Hooker, Son of, M.
Hamilton, Alexander, 280.
Hamilton, Mrs. Alexander, M.

Hamilton, Mrs. Gertrude V. C., Jr., M.
Hamilton, Lady, 261.
Hamilton, Violet, M.
Harriman, Caroll, M.
Havemeyer, F. C., M.
Henriette d'Angleterre, 231.
Henrietta Maria, 342.
Heylyn, Mrs. Ann, 141, M.
Heylyn, Mrs. Harriet, 142.
Hinckley, Mrs., 145.
Hirsch, Mrs. Julia W., M.
Hoffman, Mrs. Charles Frederick, Jr., M.
Hoffman, Mrs. George, 28, 293.
Hoffman, Mrs. Rogers, 263.
Hortense, Queen, 320.
Howes, Rev. Reuben W., D.D., 36.
Hunt, Mrs. George, 113.
Hunt, Richard, 187.
Hurlburt, Mrs. Jerome, M.
Hutton, Laurence, 182.

Jackson, Andrew M., 112.
Jackson, Mrs. I. R., 300.
Jackson, Mrs. I. R., and Mrs. John Lee, 298.
Jay, Mrs. John, 49.
Jenkins, Kathleen, M.
Jennings, Sarah, Duchess of Marlborough, 348.
Jobert, Mrs. Paul, 174.
Johnson, Mrs. R. U., 55.
Johnston, Wm. Royal, 297.
Jones, Mrs. Edward Renshaw, 121.
Jones, Mrs. Howard, M.
Jones, Oliver H., 185.
Josephine, Empress, M.

Keats, George, 274.
Keats, John, 273.
Keats, Tom, 275.
Keith, Mrs. Boudinot, 277.
Kemble, Gouveneur, 289.
Kemble, Peter, 290.
Kendal, Miss, 217.
Kennedy, E. G., 64.
King, Mrs. H. P., 250.
King, Mrs. Wm. F., 221.
Kingdon, Mrs., 27.
Knowlton, Miss, M.

Lacazette and Mlle. Desbrosse, M.
Lande, Mrs. B., 199.
Lane, Miss Anna, 164.
Lanier, Master Charles, 227.
Lauterbach, Edward, 155.
Lauterbach, Miss Florence, 310.
Lawrence, Mrs. Frank, and Lady Vernon, 179.
Lea, Mrs. Henry C., M.
Le Brun, Charles Francis, M.
Leinster, Duchess of, M.
Lewenberg, Dr., 22.
Livingston, Maria, M.
Livingston, Robert R., 279.
Livor, Miss, 54.
Lloyd, John Nelson, 323.
Lord, Mrs. H. G., 78.
Louis XIV., 256.
Louis XV., M.
Ludlow, Henry, 79.
Lupton, Frances Townsend, 311.
Lurman, Miss F., M.

Mackaye, Miss, 241.
Maillart, Mlle., M.
Marcelle, Mlle., M.
Marie Louise, M.
Marié, Peter, M.
Marlborough, Duchess of, 348.
Marquand, Henry G., M.
Marsiglia, G., M.
Martin, Miss C., 214.
McKee, Master, M.
McKee, Miss, M.
Mengs, Antoine Raphael, 211.
Miller, Mrs. J. M., 41.
Mitchell, James S., 117.
Mitchell, Mrs. James S., 140.
Mitchell, John Murray, 16.
Mitchell, Miss Maria G., M.
Mitchell, Dr. S. Weir, M.
Mitchell, Mrs. S. Weir, M.
Mix, Mrs. Elisha, 167.
Morgan, Junius S., 32.
Morris, Mrs. Alfred Hennen, 282.
Morse, Mrs. Rebecca, M.
Morton, Hon. Levi P., 31.
Morton, Mrs. Levi P., and Children, 203.
Munde, Dr., 71.
Munroe, George E., M.D., 45.

Naegele, Mrs. Charles Frederick, 229.
Napier, Gen., M.
Napoleon I., 128, M.
Newbold, Miss Anna B., M.

Oakley, Walton Livingston, 186.

Palmer, Mrs. Potter, 77, M.
Paul I. of Russia, M.
Pearsall, Alva, M.
Penrose, Katharine Drexel, M.
Perkins, Miss, M.
Perry, Mrs. Ione H., 147.
Peter the Great, M.
Philip IV. of Spain, 350.
Piccolomini, Orazio, 301.
Poor, Miss Edith, 18.
Pope Leo XIII., 61.
Porter, Major-General Josiah, 312.
Porter, Master Sidney, 249.
Portrait after Greuze, 540.
Portsmouth, Duchess of, 197.
Potter, Bishop, 156.
Potter, Miss Helen, 162.
Potter, Mrs. James Brown, M.
Pratt, Master Charles, M.
Prentice, Mrs. Henry, 213.
Prime, Anna Bard, M.

Rachel, M.
Rehan, Ada, 271.
Renwee, Miss M., M.
Richardson, Miss Betty, 346.
Robbins, Lucie Lee, 257.
Robinson, Harriet Duer, 341.
Roche, Mrs. Burke, M.
Rockefeller, Miss E., M.
Rodewald, Wm. McN., M.
Rodewald, Mrs. Wm. McN., M.

Rogers, Daniel D., 287.
Roosevelt, S. M., 88.
Rundel, Miss, 35.
Ruskin, John, M.
Russell, Miss Lillian, 132.

Sackett, Mrs. Adam Tredwell, 200.
Sage, Lucy Sinclair, 351.
Sallée, Marie, M.
Sampson, Master, 181.
Savidge, Mrs., 91.
Schenck, Miss Aleid, M.
Schermerhorn, Mrs. Wm. C., 248.
Schieffelin, Mrs. W. Jay, 246.
Schlippenbach-Schonermarck, Daughter of Count, 321.
Schwartz, Miss Julia, 154.
Seligman, Jesse, M.
Seligman, Mrs., 180.
Shelley, Percy B., 151.
Shepard, Miss Edith, 245.
Sherman, Mrs. Thaddeus, 236.
Sheridan, Richard B., 127.
Simpkins, Miss Ruth, 272.
Sinclair, Lucy, 351.
Sloan, Mrs. Samuel, Jr., 232.
Sloane, Little Miss, 59.
Sloane, Miss Lila V., 247.
Snow, Mrs. George Curtis, M.
Sprague, Mrs. Charles, M.
Stanhope, Hon. Mrs., 253.
Stanton, Mrs. Edwin, M.
Stanton, Mrs. Walter, M.

Stevens, Mrs. Albert, 84.
Stewart, Mrs. Wm. Rhinelander, 153.
Stewart, Mrs. Wm. Rhinelander, Children of, 243.
Stickney, Mrs. Joseph, M.
Stranahan, J. S. T., M.
Strickland, Miss Martha, 283.
Sturgis, Miss, M.
Stuyvesant, Mrs. Nicolas W., 107.
Sutro, Mrs. Rosa, 336.
Sutro, Mrs. Theodore, 233.

Tailer, Robert, M.
Taylor, Mabel Hayward, M.
Taylor, Master P. D., 14.
Thaw, Mrs. B., M.
Thompson, Mrs., 118.
Townsend, Mrs. David C., M.
Townsend, Elizabeth Platt, M.
Townsend, Miss M. G., 223.
Trask, Mrs. Spencer, 175.
Tucker, Miss Susie, M.
Twachtman, J. H., M.
Twombly, Miss Ruth, 226.

Vail, Miss Anna Murray, 20.
Vanderbilt, Miss Consuelo, 108.
Vanderbilt, Harold, 58.
Van der Poel, Mrs. S. Oakley, 12.
Van der Poel, S. Oakley, 11.
Van Vredenburgh, Evelina, M.
Vermont, Mme., M.
Vernon, Lady, 179.
Ver Planck, Virginia and E., 93.

Vilas, Mrs. Charles N., 170.
Villard, Mrs. H., 24.
Vitti, Mme., 52.

Walradt, Gretchen, M.
Washington, George, 239, 286, 292.
Washington, Martha, 240.
Watson, William Argyle, M.
Webling, Lucy, M.
Weeks, Renée H., 34.
Wellesley, Mrs. Gerald, M.
Wells, Miss, 157.
Wheeler, T. M., 340.
Whistler, James McNeil, 69.
White, Richard Grant, 160, 327.
White, Mrs. Richard Grant, 161.
Whitehouse, Son of Fitzhugh, M.
Williams, Miss Jeannie Jewett, 143.
Williams, Miss Mary Mildred, 228.
Willis, N. P., 1, 115.
Wilmerding, Mrs. Lucius, 85, M.
Wing, John D., 309.
Winslow, Miss., 83.
Witherbee, Mrs. Frank S., and Children, 56.
Woodward, Mrs. Wm., Jr., 230.
Wright, Mrs. George, M.

Yeamans, Shute Shrimpton, 347.
y Escosura, Leon, 120.

www.ingramcontent.com/pod-product-compliance
Lightning Source LLC
Chambersburg PA
CBHW032250080426
42735CB00008B/1085